Becky Brown

www.ShortandSweetBooks.com

Also by Rebecca Brown:

How to Study Smart Not Hard

Becky's step-by-step guide to speeding your reading, improving your note taking, and remembering it all. Fast, easy, finally!

HOW TO MAKE As in eCOLLEGE

Choose the right online schools
Earn the top grades &
Finally get the job
you deserve.

Copyright © 2007 by Rebecca Brown
Second Edition

Published By Short & Sweet Books
ISBN 978-0-6151-4464-1

All rights reserved. No part of this book may be reproduced, stored in a retrieval system, or transmitted by any form or by any means, electronic, mechanical, photocopying, recording, or otherwise, except as may be expressly permitted by the applicable copyright statutes or in writing by the author.

Contents

1: Making the First Big Decision: On-Ground or Online?   1

Questions to Ask Yourself 2
Checking Credentials   6
What is Your School's Reputation?   9
Who Are the Faculty?   12
Fees & Tuition   15

2: What is Distance Education?   17

How You "Go To Class"   18
Accelerated Classes   19
Course Load   19
Asynchronous vs. Synchronous   20
Participation Requirements   23
Vacations & Time Off   25

3: Mastering the Technology 27

The Basics   29
Newsgroups & Message Boards 30
Posting   32
Attaching Documents   35
Microsoft Office Suite   37
eCollege Software   45
Outlook Express Software   46

4: Communicating with Your School 49

How To Make As in eCollege

    Three Main Sections of Online Schools   50
    Making Friends with your Professor   52
    What to Do If You Think Your Professor Has Made a Mistake   59
    How To Contact Your Professor   60
    Navigating Administration   63
    Working with Your Academic Advisor   63
    Filing Grade Grievances 66
    Getting to Know Your Peers   68

5: The All-Important First Day of Class   73

    Introducing Yourself   74
    The Syllabus   76
    Submitting Assignments 84
    Assignment calendar
    First Day Tasks   86
    Write A Paper Criteria List   89

6: The Smartest Student does Not Get the A   93

    Check Your Weekly Grade Report   94
    How To Calculate Your Grade Each Week   98

7: How to Study Smart Not Hard   103

    Smart Notes   104
    Fast Sheets   110
    Make a Glossary of Words and Phrases   114
    The Dreaded Peer Group Assignments   116

8: Writing A Papers   121

    The Kinds of Papers You Will Write   122
    Researching Your Papers   125
    Making Annotated Bibliographies   131

9: Avoiding Plagiarism and Copyright Infringement   135

10: MLA and APA Styles   143
    What Are Styles? 145
    The Two Primary College Styles   145

Appendixes   150
    Appendix A: CHEA Recognized Accrediting Organizations as of 2006   151
    Appendix B: Glossary of Terms   153
    Appendix C: Online Resources   161

A Word From Becky

Dear student, congratulations on taking the time to pick up another book in addition to all those books you're required to read for class. I know it seems like you've already got enough work to do, but I promise you, this Short & Sweet Book is going to reduce your work load, not add to it!

First let me tell you a little secret that it took me years to discover for myself: the students who get the As in class are not always the smartest students, nor the ones that work the hardest, nor the ones that are most popular.

For the most part, the A students are the ones who have learned how to work smart—not hard!

The truth is, being the hardest working stiff isn't what gets you ahead in life. Those people out front winning the race, getting the promotions, earning the incomes, and making the grades are the ones who figured out how the system works. Then they made that system work for them.

In this book, I'm going to teach you the system

work of online schools (and most on-ground schools) and how to budget your time so that you're spending it on those things that will help you earn As and get that degree.

How to Use This Book

I hope you can find the time to read this. There is a lot of important information condensed into these few pages. The better you know it, the more easily you'll be able to use it to consistently earn the A in your class.

But you can also use this book as a reference. As you're taking a class, feel free to check the book for possible solutions to problems, answers to questions, and tips for speeding your studying and writing. The table of contents is a great place to learn what is here, and then you can focus your search on exactly the information you need, exactly when you need it.

Welcome to online school. I wish you the very best in your education. As always, I welcome your questions, comments and concerns. You can reach me at BeckyBrown@ShortandSweetBooks.com.

-Becky Brown

Making the First Big Decision: On-Ground or Online?

The most important decision you must consider before you invest any time and money in an online course of study is whether or not attending college online is the right approach for you. Yes, taking classes from your living room, in your pajamas, in the middle of the night has a certain undeniable appeal. But remember, this isn't easy college, it's only convenient college. The work load will be just as heavy as on-ground college, and quite likely heavier!

Questions to Ask Yourself

1. Can you really take the extra time away from your family and hobbies?

    Be careful when evaluating the amount of time any school or recruiter claims you will have to spend doing course work. If you are attending an accredited on-line institution, you'll likely spend **more** time on class work and assignments than you would in on-ground courses.

    Since online college classes tend to be work-intensive to make up for the fact that you don't ever sit in a classroom in front of your professor, these classes require **at least** 20 hours of work and participation each week—and much more if you hope to earn better than a C.

    That means evenings sitting in front of your computer rather than in front of your television or with your kids.

Making the First Big Decision　　3

2. Are you the sort of person who can commit himself to the requirements of online school without the extra push of in-person classes to force you to get assignments done?

   Although appealing for its accessibility, taking classes online requires that you be much more internally motivated than the average college student. You'll have to have the commitment to get yourself to class everyday (even though that just means getting to your computer).

3. Do you have the technology you need to attend online school?

   You'll have to know that you'll always have the required technology (ISP, computer, software), and that these are all reliable. Online schools are not very sympathetic to problems with your computer or your Internet connection, so be sure you have everything up to standards before you enroll.

If you answered yes to all of that, then online college might be exactly what you're looking for! The program you select should fit the kind of work and home schedule you must live with.

Consider Your End Goal

Consider what you plan to do with your degree. Although online schools are rapidly gaining in reputation in the world of higher education, many more traditional employers still prefer a traditional college.

If your employer has already given you the go-ahead with your online school, then don't sweat it! The degree you earn from UOP or Kaplan or Capella will be recognized and accepted by that employer, and likely you'll have learned as much (or more) than the on-ground student.

Look at Expectations in Your Field

If you plan to go into more traditional fields of study later on—like law or business—you certainly want to do a little research into the reputation of those schools among the professionals of that field.

For instance, all states except California require that any aspiring attorney have attended a law school accredited by the

American Bar Association or they won't allow you to sit the Bar Exam. Don't waste your time in a law school online that doesn't give you access to the only licensing examination in your state. You might be an expert in the law when you are handed your degree, but it won't get you a job as a lawyer.

When the Degree is the End Goal

For many of you, though, it is the mere lack of those two or three initials after your name which is the sole reason for missing out on promotions and remaining stuck in a job you could do with your eyes shut. If simply having the degree is what will guarantee you advancement in your field, then by all means, take advantage of an industry geared toward teaching working adults with flexible schedules and accelerated courses. There is nothing wrong with being goal oriented!

Checking Credentials

You absolutely must check the credentials of any school from which you plan to earn a degree. Remember, your degree is only as good as the school from which you got it.

What is Accreditation, and Who Decides?

The Higher Education Act of 1965 is federal legislation that provides financial support for students who want to pursue an advanced degree. The act says that if the school is accredited the federal government will provide grants and loans for students to attend it.

Since most students must take out loans to afford the ever-increasing cost of higher education, most will not be able to attend non-accredited institutions. Any school that wishes to attract students with federal loans and grants must be an accredited institution.

The Accreditation Boards

The enactment of this law lead to a number of accreditation boards throughout the

Making the First Big Decision 7

country that evaluate the quality of education any college or university sells to the public. These organizations are themselves monitored by the Council for Higher Education Accreditation (CHEA). According to CHEA, there are 19 recognized accrediting institutions in this country that review schools.

Don't Pay Top Dollar for Low-End Schools!

All this monitoring is intended to ensure that students who pay top dollar for expensive educations are actually getting value for their money. If you want to check out whether the school you are planning to attend (or are attending now) is accredited, take a look at the Council for Higher Education Accreditation website found at: http://www.chea.org/public_info/index.asp

Degree Mills & Accreditation Mills

CHEA also discusses the growth of degree mills and accreditation mills, "dubious providers of educational offerings or operations [and their accreditors] that offer certificates and degrees that may be considered bogus."[1]

These misleading institutions will sell programs or degrees that are not recognized by employers or other universities and colleges.

The result may be that you spend a lot of time and money working toward a degree that won't get you that job promotion and that can't be transferred to any other school for continued study. Not a happy thought!

Check Up on Your Own School

Appendix A is a list of all CHEA recognized accrediting institutions. It would be worth your time to ensure that your school is accredited by one of these organizations.

Reputation is More than Just Accreditation

But remember, accreditation is not the same as reputation. A degree from Harvard will always be worth much more than a degree from any community college although both are accredited, because of Harvard's ex-

Making the First Big Decision   9

cellent reputation for faculty, students, and educational programs. So the next thing you must investigate after assuring yourself that the school is accredited, is the reputation of the degree you will be paying to earn!

What is Your School's Reputation?

Of course, we all can't have degrees from Harvard (another reason it is such a desirable degree) and that doesn't mean that all other degree-granting universities are useless. Of course not!

What it means is that each institution of higher education falls on a scale of desirability. There is actually a ranking of all colleges and universities that is published each year by Newsweek that you can check out to see just where any traditional, on-ground university falls in this ranking. The higher your school ranks, the more your degree is worth to employers. The more the degree is worth to an employer, the likelier you will be hired by that employer.

How Rank is Determined

This rank is based on a number of factors, including how satisfied students and graduates of the school are with their education and degrees, how employers perceive the "clout" of that degree, the level of acclaim and education of the faculty, the kinds of programs the school offers, and many other things.

Why Schools Object to Ranking

Many schools object to this ranking system because, as they rightly point out, a school that is ranked #125 might very well give the same **quality** education as a school that is ranked at #20. But, in our world of reputations, no one can argue that if an employer sees you have a degree from Columbia they will hire you rather than the person with the degree from the local community college, if all other experience is equivalent (and sometimes even if it's not).

Online School Ranking

Many organizations are now beginning to rank online schools as well. A quick Internet search using the term "online school rank-

Making the First Big Decision

ing" will turn up several of these. While this is a good resource for evaluating the schools you are considering applying to, none of these compare the quality of the degree you earn online to a degree you would earn in an on-ground university. Thus, it is still important to know the field in which you plan to use your degree, and to understand how the professionals in that field view your online degree.

Why Should You Care About Rank?

If you are going back to school purely for the love of learning (a perfectly respectable, even admirable, reason in my book) then you shouldn't care. I believe that in most distance education institutions a student can learn just as much or more in online classes because faculty participation and student projects are much more in-depth and frequent than in on-ground classes.

However, most students do not have the leisure and financing to attend college merely as entertainment. They need their education and degree so that they can advance in their jobs or start a new career. Those students **must** care about accreditation and reputation. Once again, let me remind you that your degree is only as valuable as the school from which it comes. So in the spirit of a good consumer, do your research and be sure you are paying for the education you'll find most useful.

Who Are the Faculty?

Another good measure of a school is its faculty. Most online universities will link you to their faculty website where you can read about the qualifications of those professors who will be teaching you. As you look through the list of instructors, ask these questions:

- What degrees do the faculty have?

    Do they all have post-graduate degrees (degrees earned after the traditional B.A. from a four-year institution)?

- Do most if not all of them have terminal degrees: MBA, Ph.D., J.D.?

Making the First Big Decision

A terminal degree means the faculty member has taken his/her program of study to its highest level of completion. The faculty with the M.A. usually only had a two-year course of study in his program. The faculty with a Ph.D. has spent four years or more in her course of study.

The terminal degree means there are no more formal programs that person can take in that area of study. So although it doesn't mean there is nothing left for her to learn, it does mean she's completed more formal training than someone who only went as far as an M.A.

- *What courses do the faculty members teach? Are they teaching in the same areas in which they have a degree?*

Most institutions are quite diligent about checking that their faculty have earned quality degrees. However, many schools will hire faculty with degrees for accreditation purposes, then allow them to teach in other areas if they have taken a course or two in that subject. Do you want your professor instructing you in your major area of study when they have taken less classes in that topic than you have? Probably not.

- *How many of your faculty are adjuncts?*

Many of the online schools (and increasingly more of the on-ground schools) employ part-time faculty to teach the majority or all of their courses. There is nothing wrong with part-time faculty—they are often just as qualified and likely are more enthusiastic professors than their full-time brothers and sisters. Part-time faculty are eager to prove to the school how dedicated and valuable they are in order to earn a full-time position.

However, some schools look at this rather large group of educators as a freely available pool to which they owe no responsibility or loyalty in return. Most have no intention of ever hiring them full-time.

Since adjuncts work on contract, getting paid one fee for each class they teach—no matter how many students or how much work that class entails—many adjuncts are over-worked and poor. If they complain, the school will drop them without hesitation and hire one of the many new adjuncts just waiting to teach.

Why Should You Care About Faculty?

Why should you care if your professor is over-worked and underpaid? Well, think about this: The less a school pays an instructor for each class, the more classes he will have to teach in order to support his family. That translates into less attention for each student (that's you, my dears) and harried, irritable professors. When faculty feel overworked and uncared for by the schools where they teach, they transmit that same feeling to their students.

Wouldn't you rather be instructed by faculty who can take the time to work with you, answer your questions in detail, spend plenty of time reading and commenting on your papers because they are making enough money so they can teach fewer classes?

It's in your best interest to attend schools that treat their faculty well and value them as professional educators. The better an institution treats their faculty, the better faculty will treat you!

Fees & Tuition

According to a study conducted by the US Department of Education on distance learning and post-secondary education, "Tuition and fee charges for students in postsecondary distance-delivered courses tended to be the same as for campus-delivered classes."[2] Meaning, you pay the same, whether you drive to your campus and sit in a live classroom, or work online from home.

This isn't the cheaper alternative, it's merely the more convenient alternative. Just one more reason to expect the same quality of program, instructors, and administrators from online, distance education as from on-ground traditional universities.

---

[1] Council for Higher Education Accreditation, retrieved on 01/05/07 from http://www.chea.org/degreemills/default.htm

[2] CHEA, "Distance Learning in Higher Education – CHEA Update No. 3" retrieved on 01/05/07 from http://www.chea.org/Research/distance-learning/distance-learning-3.htm

What is Distance Education?

Distance education, also known as online university and eCollege, is a method of delivering college-level programs and courses to students who cannot sit in the same physical classroom as their instructors. These programs can be full, fifteen-week semesters just like the equivalent on-ground terms, but are more likely to be accelerated courses where all class work is compressed into between five and 10 weeks of online study.

Most schools these days are getting into the distance education game since this is such a lucrative market for educational institutions. Without the overhead cost of buildings, utilities, and campuses, and with the burgeoning new market of adult students who need the convenience of attending college from work or home, this is a big profit-making area for all schools.

How You "Go To Class"

Most schools will use software to deliver their online programs, and require that students participate in online discussions with professors and classmates while completing course work such as reading, tests, and paper writing. Some classes require you to be online at a specific time each week to meet with your professors and classmates, while others do not.

What is Distance Education?

Accelerated Classes

Online classes are generally accelerated classes. That means they encompass the same amount of reading, lectures, discussions and assignments of a traditional class but you do it all in one third of the time. A regular semester-length, on-ground course lasts approximately 15 weeks. The online course can be anywhere from five to ten weeks depending on the school.

This means, of course, that you are doing quite a bit more work each week than you would be in the on-ground classroom. But it also means you could earn your degree faster than the average on-ground students.

Course Load

However, the online student is usually only taking one or two classes at a time (traditional students take 3-5 at a time), due to the heavy workload per class. But because most schools offer courses that start every week, or at least every month, you can schedule your classes throughout holidays and summer vacation, which you can't do in the more traditional schools.

You will likely receive plenty of feedback on your assignments too, as instructors are required to evaluate substantively and frequently. So the work you do turn in will be read, commented on, and returned to you within a week—and quite a bit sooner at some schools.

If you are a motivated student, you can be improving your study and writing skills each week, and incorporating those improvements into each new assignment. Very quickly, you'll have mastered the technique of learning using this new medium and will accelerate far beyond your on-ground brothers and sisters.

Asynchronous vs. Synchronous

Asynchronous courses never require that you be online at the same time as anyone else in your class, including your instructor. The beauty of asynchronous courses is that you really can do that work any time during the day that you can fit it in, even if that is in the middle of the night.

Synchronous courses require students to meet online at a scheduled time each week. During these meetings faculty and students meet in a chat room where they can "talk" in real time. Faculty usually have lessons planned, which often include visual aids like movies, podcasts, and PowerPoint presentations. Students get to really meet their classmates, exchange comments, questions, and greetings, and get immediate responses from their instructors.

Synchronous Classes are Better

This may sound completely counter to the whole online learning experience, and many students just can't manage synchronous classes because of their complex daily schedules and demands from bosses and family. However, I recommend that if you can work in one hour a week to meet during regularly scheduled live class sessions that you do it! I teach both asynchronous and synchronous kinds of courses, and the ones that require the synchronous meeting for just one hour a week so substantially increase the understanding of students and elevates the entire distance education experience that I always recommend it.

This is Nothing Like a Correspondence Course

Don't expect online classes, asynchronous or synchronous, to be anything like a correspondence course, where you can do the reading and polish off a few assignments in a couple of hours at the end of the term. You also cannot work ahead of your classmates to get everything completed in one or two weeks.

Almost every online class requires that you work along with your classmates—usually completing several assignments and projects by the deadline each week. Some faculty might allow you to work a bit in advance of the class, say, complete the reading or write a paper that isn't due until next week. But most will not.

Online Imitates On-ground

Remember, most schools try to make the online classroom as similar to the on-ground classroom as they can. So just like a traditional college class, you will have reading assignments that relate to the projects that are due that week. Quizzes and tests will require you to know this material, and assignments are based on your learning from that week, and will be evaluated and graded each week.

Additionally, classroom participation—which in this world means writing comments and answers to discussion questions each week—is highly regarded as one of the key learning tools. So you will find varied degrees of participation are also required by each school.

Participation Requirements

Participation is how much time you spend online working on the course website. This can be calculated by actually tracking the amount of time you spend on that webpage (which many of the schools' computers automatically keep track of) or by counting the number of messages that you post on the website.

Watch Out for High Participation Requirements

Participation can be a heavy burden to handle if you are trying to minimize the amount of time you spend online. Requirements might be as steep as posting four to five **substantive** messages each day, for five out of seven days each week. Or 25 well-written, 350-word notes on assigned topics each week.

Depending on your skill with the course subject matter, and how easily you can write substantive messages, this could take you an hour a day just for the participation requirements. (This is in addition to required reading, projects, papers, tests and other assignments each week).

So be sure to find out what is required at any school you are considering, and calculate that into the time you can afford to devote to your classes each week.

Vacations & Time Off

Although at this writing most schools now take at least one week off at Christmas, this is generally the only holiday that they recognize. Because you decide when to attend class each week, schools assume you can work around all other days off. They will let you choose whether or not to participate on that day, but still require you to meet all deadlines for that week.

So if you really must have Valentine's Day off or risk loosing what little personal life you have left, feel free to take it. Just as long as you turn in your assignments and meet other participation requirements for the week.

Instructors Have Even Less Time Off

Remember, your instructor also gets the same limited vacation time each year, and she's been doing this for far longer than just the two years it takes to earn a degree. So if during the week of Thanksgiving, you feel your instructor is a bit slow grading papers, or isn't participating as much as usual, cut her a little slack, okay? She might return the favor one day.

Mastering the Technology

You can't take classes on the Internet if you don't know how to use a computer and on-line software. Really, you just can't!

So if this is your first exposure to using the Internet, emailing, posting to newsgroups and using Microsoft Word, you will simply have to invest the time (and sometimes money) into learning these new skills.

This may seem like self-apparent wisdom, but you would be surprised how many students (and even some faculty) I have met who don't factor this learning into their overall college plans, and spend many a night before a deadline tearing out hair because they can't make an assignment attach to their post.

In this chapter I give you a basic tutorial about each of the processes that are absolutely necessary for taking online classes. But this is not a complete tutorial, since each piece of software can be very complex and requires entire books of their own to explain.

This will get you through the first class, but I strongly encourage you to use Appendix C in the back of this book to find online tutorials and texts that will give you a more complete understanding of how this technology works. It is worth your time (and will save your hair) if you do.

The Basics of a Text-Based Education

At this writing, almost all online classes are text based. That means you communicate with your professor and your classmates by writing messages that are posted to public message boards where everyone in your class (and anyone who has access to your class) can read them. This is because most students do not have the high bandwidth required to to download and access very large files like video and sound. This is certainly the future of online classes, but it is not the present.

Online School is Writing and Reading

So your work will all entail typing on the keyboard of your computer and uploading what you've written to your classroom. You will also be heavily involved in reading; both what your professor has assigned you in textbooks and online eBooks, and what your professor and classmates have written.

If reading and writing are not your cup of tea, you might want to reconsider this kind of advanced education. Even with transcription software and voice recognition, there is simply no way to get around it, how you write will heavily affect your grades in any online class.

Newsgroups & Message Boards

Classes are conducted on newsgroup, which are also called message boards or bulletin boards. Newsgroups work very much like a real bulletin board. People post notes on the bulletin board and other people read those notes and post replies.

Public Spaces

Usually there will be one or two newsgroups or message boards that everyone in the class can read. So everything you write there you, your classmates, and your professor will be able to see. There also might be newsgroups or message boards that only you and your professor can see. Anything you write in these private newsgroups will be kept just between you and your professor.

It's also important to remember that anyone that has access to your classroom, such as administrators, academic counselors, your classmates' spouses and kids, can read what is posted there.

This is a **public space** and as such you should always be sure that anything you write there you want the public to read!

Archives

Everything you write in class is also archived and kept by the school. So if you lose your temper at a classmate—or <gasp> your professor—and write something you later wish you hadn't, it lives on forever in the archives of that school, and can be easily accessed by simply searching on your name.

So **beware!** This is the world of Big Brother. Don't commit anything to print that you might later regret.

Posting

Posting is how you get messages that you write on your computer up to the school's computer. When you put a message on a bulletin board or newsgroup, it's called "posting" the message. Messages on bulletin boards or newsgroups are called "posts." (Imagine that.)

The newsgroup is really just the server that the school has dedicated to your class. It's a computer in that school someplace. When you "post" a message, you're essentially sending an email to that computer, which it then displays for everyone to read (everyone who has access to that newsgroup).

No Deleting Posts

That's why once you send a post, you cannot get it back or delete it. You don't have the necessary access to delete posts from the school computer, although you might be able to delete them from your own computer. This is sometimes a hard concept for students to grasp.

> I like to explain it this way:
>
> Imagine you wrote a letter, made a copy, and sent the copy to your mother.
>
> Later, you regret the letter you sent to your mother, and you burn your copy. Does your mother still have her copy of the letter?
>
> Of course she does! Your mother still has that horrible letter you wrote to her, because you burned your copy, not her's.
>
> That's the way posting works. You are only sending a copy to the school's computer, and when you look at the newsgroups, you are only reading a copy of your post.
>
> So deleting a post from your computer doesn't delete it from the school's computer. Just because you can't see the post anymore, doesn't mean that others can't see it.

Most posting software like eCollege, doesn't even have an option for deleting posts. So be very, very careful what you send to your class.

Writing Readable Posts

Some schools allow you to edit messages that you've already posted—but many do not. And since much of your grade depends on the quality of your posts, it's very important that you proofread and revise those messages before you send them.

> **Before you hit the send button, review what you've written:**
>
> - Is it legible?
> - Do you sound LIKE YOU'RE SHOUTING?
> - Do you use capitol letters at the beginning of sentences and periods at the end?
> - or do u wrt in some knd of shrt-hand tht is herd t reed?
> - Hou is yerr speling? Our u usinng spelcheek?
> - If I saw you on the street, would I recognize you by your writing?
> - Does your writing make you look sloppy and haphazard, like a homeless person, or professional and intelligent?

Remember, nobody in this class will likely ever see your face, including your professor. They won't see that snazzy haircut you just got, or the beautiful clothes you usually wear. They won't see how polite you are at work, or what a lovely personality you have. They only see your posts!

Your posts are your face now. So think about what you want your face to look like.

Attaching Documents

When you turn in a paper or other document to your professor for grading, you will have to **attach** that paper to your post to send it. Attaching just means that when you send the post to the school's server, a copy of the paper goes along with it.

Most software programs allow you to attach a document by clicking on a button that says "Attach" or on a little paperclip icon. Once you click on that button, a window will open up allowing you to type in the name of the document or find it on your computer.

Make a Folder for Your Class

That's why it's important to remember where you saved your paper, and what you named it. A good idea is to make a folder on your computer that is just for your papers *in that class*. If you have more than one class, make a folder for each class.

Then when you save the paper, save it using your full name and the name of the assignment. Remember, your professor will be downloading a lot of papers to her computer each week to grade. If you just call your paper "Assignment.doc" how will she know whose paper that is once it's on her computer? So use your name and the name of the assignment as the document name. That would look something like this:

BeckyBrown_PersuasivePaper.doc

This tells the professor who wrote the paper, and which assignment it is for. If your professor loses your paper, you will have to re-send it at best, and at worst you might get a zero on it. So save everyone the confusion and name your assignments appropriately.

Microsoft Office Suite

Every school I know of requires that you use the Microsoft Office Suite for your assignments. The Suite includes Microsoft Word,

PowerPoint, Excel, and some other programs. Yes, it is expensive, but it is the cost of going to school. So look at it as a required investment, like textbooks. (Don't get me started on whether you **really** have to buy the books – you do if you want an A in the class.)

Microsoft Word (MSWord)

You will be required to write your papers in Microsoft Word (MSWord). This is not the same thing as Notepad, WordPerfect, or MSWorks. An MSWord file ends in ".doc" and unless you send a file that ends that way, your professors will likely be unable to open your documents. If they can't open them, they can't grade them. It's not their responsibility to figure out how to open your assignments, it's your responsibility to deliver a document in the required format.

Freeware MSWord Compatible

The good news is that there are online versions of MSWord that you can get for free. One of these is at:

http://www.aplusfreeware.com/categories/business/FreeMSWordAlternatives.html

With this software you can read MSWord documents and write documents that can be opened by MSWord applications. So you don't have to buy MSWord if you are really short on cash (or time).

Save Papers as .txt or .rtf

In fact, saving any file as "Rich Text" or ".txt" or ".rtf" will likely ensure that your prof can read the paper.

Using Track Changes to Read Comments

You also have to be able to read your instructor's comments when he sends the paper back to you. Most professors use the MSWord editing feature, "Track Changes," to write comments on your paper. If you don't have MSWord to look at those papers, then you won't see these comments and you won't be able to improve for the next assignment.

Mastering the Technology

So the final word? If you simply can't afford Microsoft Word, you can make do with one of the free applications—as long as you save the file in a version your prof can open. But in the long run you will lose out on points and grades. Considering how much money you're spending on college, is it really worth the penny saved?

MSWord Tutorials

If you need help learning to use your MSWord program, there are a number of free, online tutorials for you to use. Here are a few I like:

http://www.bcschools.net/staff/WordHelp.htm
http://office.microsoft.com/en-us/training/CR061832731033.aspx
http://www.internet4classrooms.com/on-line_word.htm
http://www.learnthat.com/courses/computer/word/
http://netforbeginners.about.com/od/learnmsword/Learn_Microsoft_Word_97_2000_2002_2003.htm

PowerPoint

This is the program that business people use on a daily basis to create visual presentations. If you haven't run across it yet in work, you will. So take advantage of this opportunity to practice using it.

Most classes use PowerPoint in some way. Since it compresses to a very small file size and can be easily converted to online presentations and even websites, it's a perfect tool for creating visual instructions to deliver to people via the Internet. You will probably be given PowerPoint presentations to help you understand materials in your courses, or it might be used in seminars and live chat sessions.

You will also likely be asked to create PowerPoint presentations for some of your assignments. Obviously, this means you need the program! I am not aware of any other program or freeware that is equal to PowerPoint, so this time you will simply have to cough up the dough and buy it.

Mastering the Technology

Because this is such a great tool, it is very easy to get started using, but can also expand to accomplish even the most difficult tasks. Therefore, I recommend you take a look at the Microsoft online tutorials to help you master this program. Microsoft Office Suite offers a whole series of courses to help you master the most basic PowerPoint skills to the most complex. They can be found at:

http://office.microsoft.com/en-us/training/CR061832731033.aspx http://www.bcschools.net/staff/PowerPointHelp.htm

These are certainly worth your time and effort. (If you want to get those As, that is.)

Excel

Excel is a spreadsheet software program that also comes with your Microsoft Office Suite. Excel helps you do all things involving numbers and calculations. Since I am an English professor, I can't help you with

Excel, except to say that it's awfully handy for when I want to make grade sheets.

But for you more math-inclined students, you'll find Excel is your best friend. Use it wisely—learn the program! Here are tutorials that I hear are quite good:

http://www.usd.edu/trio/tut/excel/
http://www.fgcu.edu/support/office2000/excel/
http://www.bcschools.net/staff/ExcelHelp.htm

Instant Messaging (IMing)

When you send a message to someone who is online at the same time as you, and they send a message right back that is called ***instant messaging (IMing).*** You and your friend are using an IM program that allows you to send and respond to each other in real time. It is live chatting, meaning you are chatting with another person (by typing messages) at the same time as they are chatting with you.

Many schools employ IMing for their faculty office hours. That way, you know at least once a week you can reach your professor live, in person, and ask questions or discuss projects. I find this to be an essential tool for my students and often wonder why more of them don't use it.

With a chat window open, a student can ask me how to do a particular project, and I can work with them one-on-one until they completely understand the materials. I can even send them images, visual tools to help them understand what I am teaching.

If you want to make the grades in eCollege, I highly recommend you download one of the free IM software packages and learn to use it. Then contact your professor every time you have a question or are puzzled by an assignment. She is there to help you and frankly, most professors I know sit bored and forlorn during their office hours, staring at an IM screen that no one ever messages from.

Where to Get Free IM Software

You can get the IM software from a number of places, including from AOL listed below. You'll need to download the free software and sign up for an IM name. You don't have to have the same kind of software as your professor to IM them. You just have to know their IM name. (Mine is ProfBecky. You can IM me too!)

http://www.aim.com/index.adp

eCollege Software

Most online schools use a piece of software called eCollege to produce and deliver their classes to students. eCollege looks like a website, with a menu on the left-hand side that links you to all your readings, assignments, quizzes, and discussions for each week. This type of website-based classroom is very nice, since everything you need is in the same place, and there are usually a lot of good visual aids to guide you.

eCollege also has tabs across the top of the page that lead you to your grade sheet, Doc Sharing, where you and your professor can upload and download extra documents for the class, a forum for live discussions, a bibliography with links to other useful websites your professor would like you to know about, and plenty of other cool stuff.

You don't need any special software to use eCollege. It is all delivered to you just like a web page; in fact, you can access your classroom from any computer with Internet access. So if you want to work from the library you can! Or from work, or from an Internet café—anyplace you can access the Web, you can access your class.

Outlook Express Software

Some schools deliver your class via newsgroups using Outlook Express (OE). Although this method of delivery is going out of style—there are now so many great new technologies that plain old newsgroups are very low tech these days—it is still a standard in some of the older schools.

OE is just a mail client that ships with most Windows-based operating systems. But in addition to picking up your mail with it, you can set up newsgroup accounts. As I mentioned in the first chapter, a newsgroup is just a bulletin board that you post messages to. Your messages go to a server at the school and anyone with access to those classes can read those messages.

OE doesn't include anything fancy like Instant Messaging, or whiteboards where you can chat and watch PowerPoint presentations at the same time. It is just a newsgroup where you post messages and read messages and post your assignments as attachments to your message. But because all you need to attend class is the OE software—it's pretty simple to learn how to use and free—this can be a perfectly acceptable course delivery method.

Proprietary Software

These days the biggest schools, like University of Phoenix, are creating their own proprietary software to deliver courses to students. So far, the technology isn't quite there. UOP has designed its software—which you access via the Web—to look and work just like Outlook Express. In fact, they used to deliver all classes using OE, and at the time of this writing students and faculty have the option of using OE instead of the web-based classes. Many do use OE, since it seems to work better than the proprietary software. But all that will change soon, I'm sure!

48   How To Make As in eCollege

Communicating with Your School

Knowing who to contact for each kind of situation you run into while going to college is very important. You can waste hours trying to get a hold of your professor for help with a password, when all that was needed was a quick call to tech support. Or spend days emailing your faculty advisor about a grade in a class, when your professor is the person who can help.

In this chapter you will learn how an online university is organized and who you should contact for each kind of situation you're likely to find yourself in.

Three Main Sections of Online Schools

In general, eColleges are divided into administrators, faculty, and technology people.

Administration

The administrators handle all the class scheduling, they decide what classes you will have to take to earn the degree you want to earn. They evaluate your past college credentials and decide if you get to skip ahead, or if you have to start from the beginning. They help you get your school loans, and take your money too!

Faculty

The faculty are the content experts who teach you the content of their classes. When you're just starting out, they are teaching you basics like writing, study habits, math, etc. As you progress, you get into more specific content areas that directly relate to the degree you're trying to earn, such as business, nursing, IT, etc. Professors are the ones who know your industry, know the theories and concepts you must learn, and have the task of teaching that to you.

Internet Technology (IT)

The technical people run the website, newsgroups, and email. They build the course web pages, assign you login names and passwords. They set you up in your newsgroups and help you with anything involving software or hardware.

The IT people are the go-to person for all your technical issues. Don't be afraid to call them immediately when you have a problem—you're paying their salary, and they are there to help you. In most cases, your professor cannot help you with technical issues and can't even give you extensions on deadlines if you have a technical issue.

So whenever you have a software problem, call the Helpdesk first!

Making Friends with Your Professor

Your professor is your friend! Yes, she evaluates your work and sometimes gives you grades you don't like, but her job in the long run is to help you understand the materials. So don't get mad if you are frustrated or confused. Instead, reach out with questions, attend seminars, IM her, and show that you are willing to work.

Professors don't think less of students that get bad grades, if those students are working hard to improve. They only give up on students who have already given up on themselves. So the more you show your willingness to try, the more your professor will bend over backwards to help.

Your Professor Didn't Write this Stuff!

In traditional colleges, the faculty create their own classes, decide what you have

Communicating with Your School 53

to read, make up assignments for you, and are generally in complete control of their classes. In online school, the faculty do not create the classes. Course developers (administration) decide what students will read. They write the tests, they make up the assignments, and they write the syllabus. The professor is restricted to teaching what the course developer tells him to teach. That means, even if you, your entire class, **and** your prof hate a particular assignment, there is nothing that he can do about it. You still have to do it, and he still has to grade it.

What Your Professor is Required to Do

Your online professor has a very rigorous schedule that he is required to follow in order to meet the evaluation standards of his school. Every online school that I've ever worked for has stringent deadlines regarding when their faculty must grade assignments, how much they must post on the discussion threads, and how quickly they must respond to emails. All of this is your school's attempt to ensure that you, the student, are getting plenty of good teaching and attention from your professors.

What Your Professor is Required to Do

- Grade your assignments within 7 days of the due date (faster at some schools)

- Answer emails within 24-48 hours of receiving them

- Post weekly grades that show your accumulative grade point average (GPA) for that class (Sometimes your online grade book keeps track of this automatically, so you can look anytime and your professor doesn't have to post anything extra.)

- Post to the discussion threads. Every school has a different rule about when and how many posts your prof needs to make. But in general, your professor is joining and guiding the conversation on those discussion threads. You should always read your professor's posts, even if they are to other students in the class. They are pearls of wisdom!

- Write substantive evaluations of your assignments, telling you what you did wrong so that you can fix that. (And hopefully, also what you did right, so you can keep doing that.)

- Hold office hours, either by being online during a certain time each week, or by being available via Instant Messenger during a certain time each week.

Communicating with Your School

> - Follow all the rules the school has set for how to grade and evaluate each student. Things like how late they can accept papers, how they must count students' participation, how many As they are allowed to give out. All of this comes from the administration, and the faculty member has to follow those rules.

Here is what all online professors are required to do. If your prof isn't doing this, then you should (politely) follow up with him.

Make this A Good Experience for You and Your Professor

Making this a good experience for you and your professor will go a long way toward earning that grade you desire. Sure, you can argue with your professor, flame them in class, send angry emails to them about grades your received, and file any number of grievances with the university and your academic advisor. But I guarantee, that won't change your grade one little bit. And it might make it worse.

At the end of the day, your professor has the job of evaluating your work. That is what she is required to do. She gets in trouble if she tells everyone what a great job they did without ever telling them what they did wrong.

And let's face it, that's why you're in school, isn't it? To learn? This is how learning works.

Grading is Subjective

But even if you don't care what you learn, and only care about the grade you earn, think about this: even with the best rubric and guidelines, evaluations are subjective. If you've spent the entire ten-week class making life a living hell for your prof, you can bet they will look hard to find any and every little mistake you've made on your assignments and mark you down for them.

And everyone knows, you can **always** find mistakes. If only for the sake of your grade, play nice!

Your Professor is on Your Side

But really folks, the truth is, your professor is on your side. I've been teaching for

Communicating with Your School

many years, at many different schools. In fact, I've taught more than 5,000 courses over my career! That's a lot of classes and a lot of students. So I know a thing or two about how professors and students think.

What Professors Think

Most professors are thinking about their last class and how well their teaching methods worked with those students and what didn't work at all. They're thinking about on how they can minimize the busy work and improve the learning with this new set of students.

What Students Think

Most students are thinking about how quickly they can get through this class while doing the least amount of work necessary to earn the best grade possible (I've been a student too). And hoping they have a professor that writes clearly and is willing to help out if they get lost.

You both want the same thing! To make this the most productive learning experience with the least amount of pointless busy work.

Your Professor is Your Partner

You and your professor are partners during your time in this class. Your professor wants to help you understand the materials, and you want to understand the materials. So it seems like there should never be any conflicts.

Make Life Easier for Both of You

If you want to make a good grade in a class, do your professor and your yourself a favor, make life easier for both of you. If you don't understand an evaluation, just ask your professor for clarification. He will be happy to give it to you.

If you didn't get a response to a post on the newsgroup, don't assume it is because your professor doesn't like you. He has a lot of messages to read and probably missed yours.
If you didn't get a response from an email—and it's been more than 24-48 hours—email again! Sometimes emails don't go through, or you had the wrong email address, or your professor meant to answer and got distracted and forgot. There is no reason for your professor to

Communicating with Your School

refuse to answer an email (unless it is inflammatory) so don't assume that's what happened.

Indeed, the best advice I can give you about your professor is to remember, he is a human being, not a computer. He makes mistakes, gets sick, spaces out, forgets, and gets his feelings hurt just like you do. So always give your profs the benefit of the doubt, they will appreciate your consideration, and that will always be in the back of their minds somewhere when they are deciding if you deserver a B+ or an A- on that paper!

What to Do If You Think Your Professor Has Made a Mistake

Yes, even big brains with Ph.D.s make mistakes! If you think your professor has, just ask. Don't ask by ranting and raving or sending long emails that explain why your professor is stupid and irresponsible for making that mistake. Just ask.

Don't assume that your professor is deliberately giving you a zero when you really did turn the assignment in on time, just ask.

Ask the way you would want to be asked if you were the professor, and you'll likely hear back "Oops! I goofed. Let me fix that right now for you."

Of course, sometimes the mistake is yours. Which is another reason to ask politely, and not belligerently—it's terribly embarrassing when you try to shame someone for making a mistake, and they end up turning right around and shaming you!

How To Contact Your Professor

Most schools do not provide a phone number for your online professor, because most schools do not provide phones for their faculty. They also don't provide them offices. So your professor is either working from home, or from his professional office, and

Communicating with Your School

it isn't appropriate for him to pass out his phone number to either of those places.

Email

That means you have to communicate using email or the message boards or IM. Remember, your professor is also working asynchronously, just like you. So don't assume that while you are online and struggling with an assignment that your professor is online too, waiting for your email.

In most cases, you'll have a lag time between when you email the prof, and when you hear back. So that means—and this is **very important**—that you can't ask a question about an assignment an hour before the assignment is due! Your prof just won't be able to get back to you in time.

Always give yourself at least 48 hours to work on your assignments before they are due, so you have time to ask questions and get the answer and make the changes!

Office Hours

Some professors have office hours, which means during those hours of the week they are online waiting for you to contact them. The best office hours are held using IM, so that you can actually have a long chat with your professor in real time.

I think everyone should take advantage of those office hours at least once during each course, to really get to know your prof. Ask questions, tell her a little about yourself, get to know each other.

There really is no substitute for live chatting, so take advantage of it. You'll create a much better bond with your professor, and the next time she is deciding whether to deduct late points from your paper because you turned it in one hour after the deadline, she'll think of that nice conversation she had with you.

Navigating Administration

The school administration keeps track of things like your overall GPA, the classes that you've completed for your degree, the number of classes you still have to take, and everything having to do with finances and school loans.

You know what? The administration is made up of human people too, and they also make mistakes! So if you are locked out of a class, didn't receive your text book, didn't get your loan disbursement, think you already took this class, or any other questions that have to do with your enrollment in this school, ask! They will be happy to check it out for you, fix it if they've made a mistake, or explain it if they haven't.

Working with Your Academic Advisor

Every school assigns their students to an academic advisor. This is the person that you work with one-on-one to help you navigate the confusing and often frustrating job of earning your degree.

Here are the things academic counselors are allowed to do:

- Help you figure out how your on-line class works; show you where to find your readings, the syllabus, etc.
- Help you understand your grade sheet and teach you how to read it.
- Give you study tips to improve your learning skills
- Refer you to academic success programs that will help you with any areas in which you are struggling.
- Contact your professors to see if there is anything you can do to make up missing or less than passing work.

Here is what your Academic Counselor cannot do:

- Change your grade in any class or on any assignment.
- Force your teacher to change your grade.
- Evaluate assignments and grade them themselves
- Require your teacher to accept late work, extend deadlines, or offer extra credit
- Let you into a class you've been locked out of for non-payment of tuition
- Let you skip classes

Communicating with Your School

Your academic advisor makes sure that you're taking the classes you should be taking, that you're passing those classes, and that your loans are paying for those classes.

Your professors will contact your academic advisor if your GPA falls below a certain grade (usually a D) and the academic advisor will contact you. They want you to complete your course of study too, and they'll do anything they are allowed to do, to help you get that GPA back up.

Remember, although the Academic Advisor is your guide and advocate through the university system, she has to play by the rules, too. So don't ask her to do anything that is illegal or unethical.

Filing Grade Grievances

On those occasions when you do find yourself in a class where you feel that you're not getting a fair shake from your professor (rare, but they do sometimes happen) you can file what's called a "grade grievance" to protest the grade you were given.

All you do is fill out a form—your academic advisor has it—that includes your explanation for why you think that grade should be changed, and file it with the school. A panel will review this form and make a final decision. That panel usually includes the chair of the department (your professor's boss) and the dean of the school (your professor's boss's boss).

No One Will Re-Grade the Assignment

It's good to keep in mind, though, that professors are allowed great leeway in how they evaluate and grade assignments. After all, they are the content expert. They know better than anyone else in administration whether you've really learned the concepts in your class or not. No one will second-guess your professor's professional evaluation of the work you turned in.

That means, if you file a grievance you don't get a new grade from a new profes-

Communicating with Your School

sor. Rather, the panel will look to see if there is any evidence of prejudicial treatment by your professor, if all your emails were replied to, if you were given adequate time to discuss this, and if your professor was *responsive* to your concerns (but not necessarily if they changed their mind or changed your grade.) If everything looks about average for a usual class, then the grade remains the same.

Contact Your Professor Instead

Grade grievances rarely result in a changed grade. In my experience, you will have much more success getting a grade changed if, in a very friendly manner, you contact your professor and ask them to take another look at that assignment.

If you can point out that you did do the things your professor said you lacked, then he might reevaluate that grade and give you a better one.

Remember how professors sometimes make mistakes? Sometimes they also make mistakes reading papers and evaluating assignments. So once again, I recommend that instead of jumping right to the dramatic act of filing a grievance with the school (something that always irritates professors, because they are forced to fill out a lot of extra paperwork and defend their actions) that you nicely ask your professor for a second look.

Getting to Know Your Peers

Your classmates can be of great assistance to you in successfully (and spectacularly) passing your classes. Remember, they are a whole bunch of people like you, adult learners with specific academic and career goals, trying to balance work, family and school. They are probably your most sympathetic allies.

Making Friends

If you make friends, your classmates also bend over backwards to help you. In my classes I am always amazed at the caring, affectionate, helpful students. They exchange IM names, tutor each other through the hard parts, proofread and copy edit for each other, and hold virtual hands when someone has had a rough week, or pat each other on the back when they've had a small success.

So turn to your fellow students first and last. Don't be afraid to open up and make friends. You'll probably see them in class after class as you go through your courses.

How Your Classmates Can Help You

Classmates can help you understand the reading by discussing the ideas for that week. In fact, that's what the discussion questions are supposed to help you do. Remember, two brains are better than one, and 20 can give you whole new insight on the subject matter.

So instead of only relying on your professor to explain the material, try to work it out together, with everyone else in the class. You'll be amazed at all the new perspectives, and might find that the ideas that surface during a class discussion will be just the ideas that earn you an A on the paper.

What Not to Say to Your Classmates (or Your Professor)

That being said, here are a few words of caution: remember that your classmates all come from different parts of the country, different backgrounds, and different life experiences. Don't expect them to see the world exactly the way you do, and don't expect them to always agree with you.

If you find that you heartily disagree with something a classmate has posted, it's okay to politely say you disagree and explain why. It is not okay to flame them! (This goes for your professor too.)

Free Speech in the Classroom

The classroom is meant to be a forum where people feel free to discuss many ideas and disagree with each other. I have seen entire classes go mute after one student flames another for an opinion with which he disagrees. After all, nobody wants to voice his or her opinions if there is a risk of being verbally attacked.

Communicating with Your School

Although we all know that saying, "sticks and stones will break my bones, but words will never hurt me" it just isn't true! Words do hurt. And they hurt a lot more if you can't hear the tone of voice with which they have been said. I have received emails and read posts that felt like a slap in the face. I've brooded for days over thoughtless and needlessly harsh comments that students and even other faculty and administrators have said to me.

Watch Out for that Tone!

The worst thing about this medium is that whatever you write stays right there for people to read over and over. So the emotions of a moment become a fixture in the classroom that is impossible to forget or ignore.

Please, please, don't write anything harsh or less than friendly in any message you send to your classmates or professor (or anyone, actually). If you feel your blood pressure rising, step away from the computer. Take a deep breath. Take a break of a couple of hours or even a day or too until you can see clearly again. Then if you must respond, respond with a very polite, very nice reply.

Likely the person that upset you is feeling bad about what she wrote too, and wishes she could take it back. Be the bigger person, and make it nice for everyone again.

The All-Important First Day of Class

It's the first day of class, and you didn't even get new school clothes! But that shouldn't dampen your enthusiasm to meet your professor and your classmates. This is not the day to play shy, or slack off and skip checking in, or just post one "checking in" post and promise yourself to read everything tomorrow.

The A student has already started reading and downloading and planning his course calendar. You should do that too! So pull out your biography, revise it from the last time you used it, and post it on the meet and greet thread and get started with the class!

Introducing Yourself

The first thing you will do with any online class is introduce yourself. In some classes you actually get graded on your introduction! For most schools, though, this is merely a way to jump-start the students, get them posting on the first day, and get them engaged with their classmates and professors right away.

Prepare Your Biography

You might want to take a few minutes to write up a short (200-300 word) biography of yourself to post for your classmates and professors. This should not be your life story. Don't start with your birth and work your way through 45 years of life! Nobody will read that.

LEAVE OUT THE PERSONAL INFORMATION

I want to warn you about writing very personal, revealing biographies. Remember, this is a professional school and these are all strangers. Although you may learn to know and even feel great affection for some of them, don't share those most intimate moments of your past with your classmates and teacher.

Don't talk about your heroine-addicted brother or your alcoholic mother, or the terrible divorce you're presently going through. Those are confessions for your diary, not for school.

The Internet is much too public a place to be exposing yourself this way. Just as you wouldn't stand up in a room full of strangers and tell them all about how you lost a child last year and have been in and out of alcohol treatment centers to cope with your relapse, you should not tell your online classmates.

I know it's tempting to pour out your secrets and send them off into the stratusphere, but there are real people reading this bio. So keep it friendly but superficial.

Instead, think of a pleasant, clever way to talk about who you are and why you're in this class. Remember, these people will never see your face or hear your voice, yet we are all human beings that need to have a picture of some kind in our minds when we communicate with others. So **write** a picture for your classmates.

The Syllabus

The first thing you'll need to do (after you post your biography) is to download, print, and **read** the syllabus.

Print the Syllabus!

I recommend printing it out, even though you can always access it on your computer. If it's in print, on your desk, you'll be much more likely to check it when you have a question or start to wonder when that next project is due.

Above all else, you want to minimize the busy work—that means arranging everything so

The All-Important First Day of Class 77

you are at your most efficient. So put that syllabus on your bulletin board, in the giant clip next to your computer, or at the front of the three-ring binder you've created for this course so you can get to it quickly.

Read the Syllabus!

Now take out your post-its and start reading the thing.

What? Read the syllabus? Am I mad?? Don't they all say the same thing?

Absolutely not! The syllabus is your contract with your professor. You must read it so you know what your professor expects of you, and what you can expect of your professor.

The syllabus tells you the textbooks that are required, the assignments that you'll be doing, the reading and the deadlines, and the late policy, grade rubrics, and a myriad other important information.

Sure, if you don't care about your grades, go ahead and rely on your prof to remind you when assignments are due. Sometimes that works. (Not in my classes, of course. I never remind anyone because all my students are adults. I know that adults take responsibility for their own work. They're spending big bucks on school and they make sure that their money is well spent by knowing exactly when everything is due.)

What to Do While You Read the Syllabus

Don't do your nails, watch the game or fix dinner. As you read your syllabus, you'll want to be doing a couple of things: noting the class rules, and writing your Assignment Schedule.

As you follow the steps below, I want you to have a pad of Post-Its next to you, so that when I tell you to, you can write a note and post it in your syllabus.

Step 1: Understand the Class Rules

You want to understand the rules for each new class. Although universities have general rules that govern things like midterms and attendance, each professor can have his own

The All-Important First Day of Class

rules about if assignments can be turned in late (the Late Policy) and how many points are deducted for those late assignments; whether extra credit is offered; whether assignments can be redone if you get a bad grade, and many other extremely important facts.

The A student learns all these rules and policies on the first day of class so that she doesn't make a rookie mistake like missing a deadline, or counting on extra

> **READING INSTRUCTIONS**
>
> It might seem self-evident that you should read the instructions in order to understand the task or assignment. And yet, so many students never take the time to do that. In their eagerness to get on with the assignment, they skip over the most important part!
>
> The A students doesn't skip anything. He knows that if the professor has taken the time to write this down, it's worth reading. So the A student knows that the rough draft must be posted in APA format and sent as an attachment, while the C student didn't realize that and loses points because the paper is not formatted correctly.
>
> Always read the instructions. No instruction is so minor it can be ignored.

credit to pull up her grade when, as it turns out, that prof doesn't offer extra credit.

Know the Late Policy

Put a sticky note by the late policy in the syllabus. Then **read** the late policy so you can be sure you understand it.

Every instructor will have a late policy. It is either a policy dictated by the school, by which the instructor must abide, or it is a policy they create and enforce themselves. I recommend you do everything in your power not to turn in assignments late.

Aside from loosing points for turning in late assignments, most classes are constructed so that each assignment builds on the last. If you skip one, or start getting behind, you'll find it impossible to understand or complete the next. Each week gets worse and worse.

Extensions on Assignments

Most professors have had enough dealings with students to know how tempting it can be to tell a really tall tale in hopes of getting an extension on an assignment or forbearance on late penalties.

Most students are amazed to find out that we hear these stories four or five times **a week.**

The Ever-Mounting Pile of Late Assignments

On the few occasions when I have offered forbearance on late assignments and allowed students to get very far behind in their class work, I've regretted it. Assignments are like bills, it only takes being behind on a couple to start weighing on even the most diligent of us—it just keeps mounting and mounting, until it is an un-scalable mountain of work.

The Student Who Gets an Extension Usually Never Turns in that Assignment

Typically, the student who gets more than a week behind on class work can never catch up. I discovered the hard way that I am doing my students no favor to let them turn their work in late. It's better to complete assignments as due. So find out on day one if your professor allow extensions, and what kind of rules she may have about using them.

Office Hours

Put a sticky note on the page by the office hours so you know when you can reach your prof.

Contact Information

Put a sticky note next to your prof's email address and IM name (write the email address on the sticky so you can read it without opening the syllabus!

Participation vs. Attendance

Every class I have taught online has been governed by two imperatives: participation and attendance. And everyone finds them confusing at first!

Attendance

Most schools keep track of whether or not students are attending class by hav-

The All-Important First Day of Class

ing their computers register every time you post something in a newsgroup or on a thread. That is attendance.

Students are usually only required to post 2-3 times each week to meet the requirements for attendance, and so remain in the class. If a student stops posting, and doesn't post for a minimum number of days, she can be dropped from the course.

> IMPORTANT NOTE: schools can rarely tell if you've just popped onto the class and looked. You have to **post something** to register attendance with the school's computer.

Attendance has nothing to do with your professor or your grade—it's something the school keeps track of.

Participation

However, participation is part of your grade and is evaluated by your professor. Participation means how much you post to the discussion threads and how substantive and detailed those posts are. You

do not earn participation points for completing and turning in assignments.
So you need to find out what the participation requirements are and make sure you meet those each week.

First Day Tasks

Now that you've read and understood all the rules, it's time to get started on the organization for this course. You need to organize your time for the entire length of the course on the first day if you want to be sure you're on top of all the deadlines and don't make any rookie mistakes like missing a due date.

Start Your Assignment Calendar

The most important thing you need to do today, the first day of class, is make your **Assignment Calendar**. (See inset)

The best way to do this is to print out an actual blank calendar that you can write on. Then as you go through the syllabus week by

Five Steps for Writing Your Assignment Calendar

STEP 1. Write down the title of the assignment on the date it is due on your calendar.

STEP 2. Next to that, write how many pages the assignment is (or the word count)

STEP 3. Now estimate how long you think it might take you to do that assignment. You'll get better at guesstimating this as you take more classes and do more projects. So start by guessing high:

> Persuasive Paper, 3500-3700 words,
> 4 days research
> 2 days writing
> 1 day revising.
> Total = 7days

STEP 4. Now that you know how much time you will likely need to complete the project, count backward from the due date and mark on your calendar when each of these deadlines should be met.

> One day before the due date, you have to be revising the paper. Two days before that, you have to start writing the paper. Four days before that you have to start researching the paper.

> STEP 5. You should now have the title of the assignment on the due date, and the words "start researching, start writing," and "revising" on the deadlines before the due date.
>
> Do that for every assignment in your syllabus and what you'll have is a great little calendar not only full of the due dates for each assignment, but a schedule for completing each part of each assignment.

week, you can write in the name of the assignment on the date it is due in your calendar. That way you know if you are falling behind and need to work late and catch up, or have a little extra time and can take a break and go to the park with the kids!

Write A Paper Criteria List

It always surprises me when I get a paper from a student that has little or nothing to do with what was assigned. I used to ask myself "Are they just turning in any old paper, and assuming I'm not reading them so won't know the difference?"

Then I discovered that they weren't carefully reading the requirements for each assignment and so they weren't being careful to meet those requirements in their papers.

If your boss asks you to send out letters to the board of directors changing the meeting time from Tuesday to Thursday, and you send out a couple of letters to some share holders, and you say the meeting has been changed from Monday to Friday, do you think your boss will be happy? Likely not!

You Don't Get Credit for Trying

You won't even get credit for doing part of the job since you didn't accomplish the goal of this task (informing the Board of the new meeting time).

The same is true in school. Unfair as it may seem, you are graded for the product you create, not the effort you put into it. So if you find yourself laboring over an assignment, take a breather and see if there is a smarter, faster way to do it.

Your Professor Grades How Well You Achieved the Criteria

Each project is designed to help you practice the skills and concepts you've learned in the class that week. So each project has special requirements that you must follow. Your professor will be evaluating your work based on how well you met the requirements for that project.

To prevent any mistakes and ensure that you meet all requirements for your paper, you must write a **Criteria List** for each assignment.

So . . . Writing the Criteria List

At the beginning of each week, take a look at the project that is due that week. Make yourself a numbered list of the requirements that you will have to meet. (See inset box.)

Now that you have this handy list, you can start planning your paper. Keep checking the list to see that you're remembering to do everything. When you've finished your first draft of the paper, check it against this list again to make sure you've done everything you should. Pretend you're the pro-

The All-Important First Day of Class

> ## Persuasive Paper Criteria List
>
> 1. Must be 2500-3500 words
>
> 2. Must be in APA format
>
> 3. Must use 3-5 sources
>
> 4. Only 2 sources can be from the Internet
>
> 5. Can't use Wikipedia at all!
>
> 6. Must be on an approved topic (have to get approval from prof by day 2)
>
> 7. Must use the concepts we've been discussing in class
>
> 8. Must incorporate peer review comments in final draft
>
> 9. Due in the dropbox on Weds of next week!!

fessor—be hard on yourself! Make yourself rewrite anything that you've done wrong.

If you make a Criteria List and check it twice (or three times), you'll at least know that you won't lose any points for foolish mistakes like posting your paper to the thread instead of the dropbox, or not using APA style when you format it.

The Smartest Student Does NOT Get The A

The A student gets the best grades in the class not because she was worlds better than everyone else in class, but because she was a tiny bit better than anyone else.

Most students (the ones who get Bs and Cs) think that A students must be brilliant scholars, much smarter than the average student. But the truth is, the difference between an A and a B is often very small. A matter of degrees. A matter of detail.

The Devil (and the A) is in the Details

The A student always reads the directions carefully so that she is following them exactly. She proofreads so that her papers are free of all typos and other errors, and she makes sure her formatting is correct.

In other words, almost anyone can get an A, if they pay attention to the little details that the B and C students never do. In this chapter, I'm going to tell you what those details are, so that you can give them the attention that the A student does.

Check Your Weekly Grade Report

The first thing you must always do is check your grades. Check the grade you earn on your assignments, check your weekly grade, and check your GPA for the entire course as it changes with each new assignment.

You should also be checking your overall college GPA, since some employers want to know what that is. But what I really want you to get into the habit of doing, is knowing exactly where you stand from day to day.

Don't Be Surprised by Your Grades

The A student is never surprised—he knows how he's doing in every class, at any given moment, and so he knows if he needs to exert himself a little more to pull his grade up, or if he can afford to take a break and watch that game.

Check the Grade on Each Assignment

Check the grade you receive on each assignment. Don't be afraid to look! Even if it is painful at first, you **must** know how you did in order to know how to improve.

Read Your Professor's Comments

Read the comments the professor makes. The feedback your professor gives you is exactly what you have to do to next time (wasn't that nice of her to just tell you?), so use them and understand them.

This isn't about punishment—this is how college works. You try something, the professor tells you what worked and what didn't, then you try something else. Eventually, you'll be writing A assignments all the time.

Use Your Professor's Comments

> A Punch List is something contractors write at the end of a long project. It's a list of mistakes that have to be fixed before the client will pay him.

So take those comments from your prof and write yourself a "punch list" so you can be sure to make those corrections on your next assignment.

Double-Check Your Grade

Then check that she's added up your points correctly and that if there is a grade, it is the right one for that amount of points, or if a percentage, that the percentage was worked out correctly. Always do this for every assignment.

Even Professors Make Mistakes

Here's another secret: even college professors can be bad at math! I am quite terrible at math and rely heavily on a calculator to help me work out the grades for my students. Even so, and although I am very careful, I have still been known to make a mistake or two. And if my student didn't catch it, I probably wouldn't have known to change it.

Do Your Own Math!

So don't be a trusting fool! Check your professor's math—make sure the addition and subtraction are right. Make sure he's given you the grade you earned. Point out nicely if he's made a mistake. Profs don't mind changing grades if it's their mistake, so don't be afraid of that.

How To Calculate Your Grade Each Week

If your professor doesn't provide you with a letter grade each week, it's very easy for you to figure it out for yourself. First, you'll need to get out your syllabus and find the *percentage to grade conversion chart*. Every school provides this. It is a chart that tells you what letter grade you will get for a percentage you've earned in class. It's usually in your syllabus, but if it's not there, just ask your prof.

$$\frac{\text{Number of points you've earned so far}}{\text{Number of points it is possible to earn so far}}$$

If your professor only gives you a point value for each assignment, there is a simple mathematical formula for figuring out what percentage you've earned so far. Take the total number of points you have earned so far in the class, and divide it by the total number of points it is **possible** to earn so far.

The Smartest Student Does Not Get the A

This gives you your score as a percentage. Then look on the percentage to grade conversion chart to see what grade that is.

> ### Check Your Grade
>
> If I earned 25 points total for weeks one and two, and it is possible to earn 30 total for weeks one and two, then my grade so far as a percentage is 83%.
>
> $$25/30 = .83 \text{ or } 83\%$$
>
> Then I look on my grade conversion chart to see that an 83% is a B:
>
> | 100-95% | A | 82-80% | B- | 69-66% | D+ |
> |---------|----|--------|----|-----------|----|
> | 94-90% | A- | 79-76% | C+ | 65-63% | D |
> | 89-86% | B+ | 75-73% | C | 62-60% | D- |
> | 85-83% | B | 72-70% | C | Below 60% | F |
>
> * Remember, each school uses their own grading scale, so you have to get the grade conversion chart from your school to find your grade. This is just an example.

Why Calculate Your Grade Each Week?

The A student knows what grade he's earning from week to week in any given class. He does not wait until the last week to wonder if he's earning an A. He already knows! That means he's so on top of watching his grade sheet that he also knows if he's slipping below that A each week.

Why is that important? Because if you see your weekly grade slip below an A, then you can start **immediately** to change what you're doing to get the grade back up.

Every grade you earn on every assignment averages into your final grade. And the more assignments you complete, the harder it will be to change your final grade.

It's Easy to Change Your Grade at the Beginning of the Course

In the first few weeks, if you miss an assignment or get a bad grade on an assignment, you can see your grade change from an A to an F very quickly! But you can change it back to an A pretty quickly too.

Not So Easy Near the End of the Course

But by the time you're into the last few weeks of classes, you've completed so many assignments, that each assignment has less of an effect on your final grade. That means the grade you're presently earning becomes very hard to change.

That's why it's important to always know what grade you're earning and work immediately to improve it if you drop below your target grade. Don't tell yourself it's okay because you have 8 weeks to go. By the time you've reached the 5th week, it will be very difficult to raise your grade at all.

Submitting Assignments

Each week you will be asked to complete and submit assignments based on the learning for that week. Aside from following directions and meeting the criteria for each individual assignment, there are some very basic guidelines you should follow when submitting an assignment.

First, assume that all assignment should be pasted into the body of your post and not submitted as an attachment unless the directions specifically tell you otherwise.

Attachments Carry Viruses

Attachments carry and transmit computer viruses, so they can be difficult to handle. Attachments that are transmitted through a dropbox (which you find in eCollege software and some others) are cleaned before being downloaded, so the viruses are wiped off them if they had any.

For this reason, it's always better to only submit attachments when your professor specifically calls for them.

Styles and Formatting Require Attaching

Any document that has to have MLA or APA or other specific formatting **must** be an attachment, since those formatting requirements can't be done on a post.

When you do attach a file, be sure that you have used a logical name to save it. That file name should include your first and last name, and the name of the assignment:

Becky_Brown_PersuasivePaper.doc.

That way, when your professor downloads your file, she doesn't end up with 15 documents called "mypaper.doc"!

Always Turn in Your Best Work (Even for Rough Drafts)

Also remember that any assignment you submit for a grade must be the best product you can create to date. That means no typos, no spelling errors, no strange line breaks or extra pages, no annotated notes left over from when you were proofreading it. It should be a clean, beautiful, perfect paper that you are proud to put your name on.

How To Make As in eCollege

How To Study Smart Not Hard

I have a whole book devoted to study habits; they are just that important! The way you study has everything to do with what grade you'll earn in a class. I've learned this all by trial and error. I have spent late nights reading, underlining, taking notes, highlighting, burning the midnight oil, all to earn a C in class. I have also read swiftly, taken Smart

Notes, and compiled Fast Sheets in one third of the time—and gotten As every time!

For the full "Study Smart Not Hard" program, you'll want to check out my book **How To Study Smart Not Hard (and Still Get an A)**.[1] But here is a quick lesson you can use right now.

Smart Notes

Don't spend hours and hours reading and rereading material that makes no sense to you! That's not smart, it's just hard.

Instead, follow these simple directions for taking smart notes that will help you read, understand, and remember!

STEP 1: Chapter Overview

1. Start by reading the Table of Contents for the chapter you've been assigned to read.

The table of contents is a great place to get an overview of what each chapter and section is about. I always start with the table of contents in any book I have to read, so I know what's coming, and have some idea what to expect. I get my mind ready to absorb that material.

2. Write in the margin next to the chapter you're going to read, what it's about in your own words.

It's very important that you actually write this by hand, and that you do it in your own words. One way you learn is by rephrasing things. It forces you to think about something, rather than letting it go in your eyes and out your ears without ever sticking to your brain! So putting an idea into your own words helps you learn it.

WHY WRITE BY HAND?

The reason you actually write by hand is that doing something physical while trying to learn, helps you learn! Physically writing those ideas down is speeding your learning.

Later, when you will type up these notes, that is another, different kind of physical activity and that too will add to the speed with which you learn and remember.

If you don't want to mark your book, write on stickies and stick them to the appropriate places in the book. That's still writing after all.

Here's an example of what that little note might look like:

"This chapter is about the First Amendment"

Easy, right?

3. Next look to see if there are any sub-headings for that chapter.

If there are, write next to each sub heading what that section is about. Here's what that might look like:

"This section is about the Free Speech clause."

"This section is about freedom of the press"

"This section is about the establishment of religion."

4. Now turn to that chapter and read the first paragraph and write in the margins next to it the main idea of this chapter.

You should only have to read the introductory paragraph to know what the main idea is, although sometimes you have to read a couple of paragraphs—just don't read too much! Write your short synopsis right next to that first paragraph.

If the first paragraph looked like this:

"The First Amendment of the Constitution guarantees some rights that our founding fathers believed to be essential to a free and functioning democracy. Those are the freedom to express yourself, the freedom of the press to write about what they want, and forbidding the government to establish a religion."

You would write something like this:

"First Amendment guarantees freedoms essential to democracy, expression, press, no established religion."

5. If your chapter is divided into sections and subsections, do this for each of them.

Only read as far as it takes to figure out what each section is about. It shouldn't take more than 10 minutes total to quickly jot down your synopsis on the page next to that section, for all sections.

6. Once you have those jotted down you're ready to transfer those notes of yours to a piece of paper.

Don't condense this step with the ones above. The more times you write something, the more you press that into your memory, like pressing a stamp into a piece of clay. The more times your press, the deeper the impression it makes, and the longer it stays. And keep writing by hand at this point.

Start with the notes you wrote in the table of contents. You're making an outline of what you're reading. Then transfer the notes you made in the chapter, putting your new notes right under each of your old notes so you can see the chapter headings and the annotations.

Step 2: Doing the Reading

Now that you've done that, go back and start reading the whole chapter word for word.

Think About What You're Reading

You already know what the chapter will be about, you know the main points the author will make, and how he has organized it. And you know what each section will be about. So you should be able to read without being too confused or puzzled.

Highlight Important Points

As you come to a sentence that you think is particularly important, you can highlight it or put a checkmark next to it. But mostly, you should just be reading and thinking about what you've read.

Transfer Your Notes

When you finish reading the chapter, go back and transfer anything you've highlighted or checked onto your Smart Notes page. If you copy anything word-for-word from the text, be sure to put it in quote marks and write the page number next to it, because if you use it in a paper later (and these Smart Notes will come in very handy when you're writing papers) you'll have to write a citation for it, so you'll have to be able to find it again.

Take a Break!

Now put away your books and go do something else. Watch the game, fix dinner, or take the kids to a movie. Stay away for at least 2 hours. When you come back to studying, first read over your notes again carefully thinking about what you read. You will be amazed at how much you remember.

Fast Sheets

Fast Sheets are cards or compiled notes that you keep handy while you work on assignments.

> In the old days we called them cheat sheets, because some baddies tried to take them into class and cheat off them during tests.

But educators have learned how important these kinds of condensed notes are for helping students learn the material and review when it's test or paper writing time. And in eCollege, where almost all tests are open book, you can use them in your tests, too!

In this step you're going to take your Smart Notes and make some Fast Sheets.

Condense Your Smart Notes

Start by taking all your Smart Notes from the week. If you had a lot of reading to do, there might be a lot of notes. You need to condense them into a more manageable size, say one or two typed pages—but no more!

As you've been reading this week, attending seminars or discussing these ideas in class, you'll find that everything has started making more sense to you. Your mind has had time to absorb the new ideas. You might have pondered them while driving to work, and maybe even had an insight or two.

Certainly if you were asked to write any discussion questions or chat with your classmates, you would have understood even better what you were reading about. And maybe someone on a discussion thread had something intelligent to say that you hadn't thought of.

Type Up Your Fast Sheets

Now is the time to incorporate all of that into your Fast Sheets. Date a new document in MSWord, and put the subject of that week's studying at the top of the page. Then transcribe your handwritten notes onto your computer page.

As you type, make changes that are necessary; if you suddenly realize that you'd misunderstood a point, make those corrections in your notes. If you thought of something clever (or if someone in class said something clever) type that into your Fast Sheet notes.

Save the Fast Sheets to Your Course Folder

Finally, save it all in your course folder, but also print off a page to read. For some reason, reading the piece of paper triggers a different neurological response from reading the screen. So you'll have one more round of learning, understanding, and pressing these ideas into your brain, which will further help you remember those concepts.

Show Your Professor that You Know the Material

It's not enough to learn the material—that's not going to get you an A.

Say what?

That's right, you might know the Constitution inside and out and still fail the class if you aren't able to convey that knowledge to your professor. You have to start using those new theories, concepts, and data in what you're writing on the discussion threads and in your assignments.

Use the Concepts in Your Writing

One of the ways you show your mastery of the material is to be able to speak and write about those ideas using the language of that discipline or profession.

> Every discipline, every profession, has its own terminology for talking about itself.
>
> When you are learning to be a writer, you have to learn the difference between proofreading and copyediting, and you have to be able to talk about those things, using the correct words.
>
> If my plumber said, "hand me that thingamajig that I use to unloosen these pipes." I wouldn't have much confidence in his ability to fix my plumbing.

In the same way, you need to master the language and terms of the subject you're studying. When you are learning about anthropology, you have to be able to discuss "artifacts" and "social systems"; when you are learning the law, you have to be able to speak of "rules" and "holdings" and "arguments."

Make a Glossary of Words and Phrases

The words and phrases that you use when writing are extremely important for showing your professor that you've learned this material. So as you read and take notes, remember the words those authors used to discuss the ideas, and use the same words and phrases when *you* discuss them.

Keeping a glossary where you can write down the new words and phrases as you encounter them will be a handy tool for when you need to use them in your writing. You can even add a mini glossary to the bottom of every Fast Sheet for each week, so when you're writing or answering questions, you have those terms right there to pop in. You'll be amazed at how intelligent you sound—quite instantly.

Try to Apply What You've Learned in Theory to Your Own Ideas

The truly brilliant student will take the ideas, theories, words, and phrases that they've been reading about and apply them to their own ideas or situations. When a professor sees this happen, he is guaranteed to be thrilled!

The way to do this is to think about how these theories or ideas might affect your life. If we didn't have the First Amendment, how would you be affected? Would you be worried about things you say on the telephone? Would you be afraid to criticize the government? When you can apply these theories to new situations, ones you haven't been reading about, you have truly learned them. Indeed, the whole purpose of paper writing is so students can apply these ideas to new situations.

BUILDING A WORKING TEAM

Your team needs to be put together like a football team; every player is assigned a different necessary task based on their personal strengths.

Is someone a born organizer? Make her the team leader. Is someone an expert with grammar and spelling? He's your copyeditor. Got somebody who loves researching online, assign her the task of digging up resources.

You get the picture. Use your collective talent wisely. Don't just divide the paper into five sections and assign each person a section—that's the fastest route to a D!

The Dreaded Peer Group Assignments

Yes, we all hate them. It seems like they are designed so that slackers will get As for doing nothing, and those of us who care about our grade end up having to do all the work. But what I tell my students when they complain is, unfortunately, this is just like real life!

Why All Colleges Require Them

Sometime in the 1980s a group of educators ran some studies and decided that the best way for students to learn was using small groups of their peers to complete team assignments.

I know how hard it is to make this work online, because every time I go through a training program, I have to do a peer assignment too! But if you follow these tips you'll find working with your team can be fun and productive.

EIGHT STEPS FOR AN EXCELLENT PEER GROUP ASSIGNMENT

1. Start immediately, on the very first day of the assignment so you have enough time to get it all done. Everything will take three times as long as if you did this assignment yourself, so you must take that into consideration or one of you will end up desperately doing all the work during the last hour of class before it is due.

2. Assign roles for every member of the group. This is not a democracy, this is a group assignment. So you must have a group leader and assigned tasks with stated deadlines. The only voting you should do should be to decide who is your team leader and what your assigned tasks will be.

3. Write a document that everyone can see (post it in your newsgroup if you can) that contains the Criteria List, the tasks for each team member, and a Task Calendar for everyone.

4. Your deadline for completing those tasks should be two days before the assignment is due.

5. Your deadline for finishing the revision of the project should be 24 hours before the project is due.

6. Your deadline for finishing the proofreading and copyediting of the project should be at least 4 hours before the project is due.

7. The team leader should be the one person responsible for turning in the final project.

8. Make sure everyone's name is on the project, even if someone didn't do any of the work. Remember to keep your eye on the goal: the grade that you earn. None of these classes are graded on a curve, so it doesn't affect your grade if someone gets a grade she didn't earn. And it will probably be the only good grade she makes in the class. In the mean time, you'll look good for building a team that really pulled together (that's what your professor will think).

---

[1] You can find the ***How To Study Smart Not Hard*** Becky Brown study guide on the Short & Sweet Books website: www.ShortandSweetBooks.com.

Writing A Papers

For most college courses, you will be assessed by the quality of papers you write for class. That's good for natural born writers, and bad for the rest of us! Because no matter how well you know the material, if you can't write about it well, clearly, and thoroughly, you won't get an A in the course.

So knowing how to write an
A paper is essential.

Kinds of Papers You Will Write

The first thing to determine when asked to write a paper is the kind of paper that's called for. Sometimes the professor will tell you. "This needs to be a persuasive paper that makes a claim and supports it with data and a strong argument."

But most often, nobody says anything about the kind of paper they want. They just tell you how many words you need, and how many sources, and sometimes what your topic will be. But they say nothing about whether you'll be arguing a point, or explaining a situation, or writing an opinion.

How To Figure Out What Kind of Paper You're Supposed to Write

The truth is, there are really only three main kinds of papers you can write, and it's pretty easy to figure out which kind is called for depending on the instructions you're given.

If you're asked to write a paper about the Constitution and **how** it was written, you're probably going to write a "how" paper, otherwise known as an Informative paper. In other words, you focus on the history and the facts. You tell the reader how it all happened, but you don't express an opinion about it.

If you're asked to write a paper about **whether** or not you think the press has too much freedom, then you are supposed to write a persuasive paper. Persuasive papers are essentially arguments. They present one point of view, and try to persuade the reader that their point of view is the right point of view. Persuasive papers depend on claims, sometimes also called opinions, and data to back up that claim.

Finally, if you don't have to provide any data to support your claim, then you are just writing an opinion piece (like an OpEd). That is, your prof just wants to hear what you think and why. But you don't have to provide evidence.

Informative Papers

The informative paper tells how to do something, or how something works, or how something happened. It's all about how. The goal is to inform your reader, but not to argue a position or a point.

When you write an informative paper you want to do research to provide good data about your topic. And you want to explain things thoroughly. But in the end, you're not trying to win an argument. Papers about how to protect children from on-line predators, how to winterize your car, why recycling can affect the weather patterns are all informative papers.

Persuasive Papers

Persuasive papers are essentially arguments. You pick a controversial topic with at least two sides, and you write an argument for one of those sides. Persuasive papers use data and experts to help persuade their reader that the paper's claim is right, and the opposition's claim is wrong.

Examples of persuasive paper topics are, why we need to take global warming seriously, why children shouldn't be allowed to use the Internet unsupervised, why the press should always be allowed complete freedom for everything they write.

The persuasive paper is opinionated, but also uses lots of research with good data and expert opinions to show the reader that the opinion is right.

Researching Your Papers

All papers for college (except fairly simple opinion pieces) require authoritative reasoning. That means you have to use **authorities**, experts in the field you're writing about, to provide you with the data and opinions for your papers.

Your personal opinion is required too. But it cannot be the whole story, because just like a kid who's told the there is no Santa Clause, the reader always wants to know "How do you know that? Who told you so? How can you be sure?" So everything you write needs to be founded on good research. Your job as the scholar is to dig up those authorities, so when your professor says, "How do you know that?" you can answer her with a list of credible sources that agree with you!

Looking Online

Where do you find these authorities? Well, in the library, of course! Just like when you were a kid. You can go to the library in your town, talk to the reference librarian, and search through stacks of books and archives of magazines and journals. Or you can open your laptop and start your research online!

Online Libraries

These days, most schools have vast online libraries that you can access from the school website with your school password. This is the best place to start your research, because most of the sources for data and opinions that you find here have already been vetted and pass the approval of your school and its professors. So you can generally trust that these are credible sources.

The Internet

But if you don't find what you need in the school's online libraries, you can always turn to the vast Internet. (NOTE: Please contact your professor to be sure that using the Internet is okay. Some professors don't allow it.) As you know, the Internet is an enormous resource of opinions and data about almost anything you can imagine. So you'll have no trouble finding something about whatever you're researching.

Use Reliable Sources

But this enormity has its drawbacks. Anyone can publish a blog, or post a comment, or even an entire website. That means checking for the reliability of your sources is essential! You don't want to fill your paper with sources that turn out to be some crackpot living on the beach someplace, do you? (Trust me, you don't! Professors look at the quality of your sources, and you loose points if they are not reliable.)

That means, although you might find a white supremacist that thinks we should bring back slavery, it wouldn't be accurate to say that most Americans want a return to the antebellum days because you read this one source! Beware the sources you use in your paper.

Use Search Engines

How do you find these pub-

What are good, reliable sources? Here's a general list:

- Sources from your school's online databases
- National publications (NY Times, Washington Post, Newsweek, Harpers, Communication Arts)
- Journals (These are published by professional organizations, and so have editors who check facts and make sure the data is accurate.)
- Government websites (for the most part)
- National high profile non-governmental agencies (like the Red Cross, Doctors Without Borders, American Bar Association) Basically, the more high-profile, the more likely you can trust their data, since a lot of people are watching them, and pointing out errors.
- Local publications are okay too, but watch out for local biases.

lications? Well, you use a search engine, of course! Any one of the available search engines like Google, Ask.com, Yahoo is fine. They all turn up pretty much the same websites. So you can just learn how to use one, and stick with it for all your searches.

The important thing to know about search engines is that they give you back lists of websites that seem to match the words you put in their search box. The closer the match, the higher up on the list that website will appear. That means the ones at the top of the list are pretty near an exact match to whatever you typed in the search box.

Try Many Different Search Words and Phrases

So do more than one search! Try many combinations of words, and use several words together—never just one word. That will get you a vast number of websites that are only generally on topic.

Using Search Terms

The way Google and other search engines work is they search the actual text of every website looking for the exact combination of words you typed into the search box.

You have to be sure that you are using a good combination of words, and that you try many different combinations so that you can find the articles you really need.

For instance, if I want to find out about the effects of global warming on the West Coast. I could just type

"global warming"

in the search box and see what I get.

But I will get hudreds of pages, each full of lists of every website that mentions the phrase global warming somewhere in their text! Not very close to the exact topic I'm looking for.

So I'll narrow that search by typing

"global warming California"

in the box, since that's exactly what I'm looking for. Now I'll only get a few dozen pages, but my list will have only websites that talk about global warming in California.

Keep Searching Until You Start Seeing the Same Sources Over and Over

Try several combinations and ways of saying something in order to find all possible articles on that subject. Each will return some different websites. But you will start to see the same articles or websites repeated. Then you know those are all about this topic. Those are probably your best sources for your paper!

Making Annotated Bibliographies

As you search for sources you should be keeping a bibliography. It will save you much more time to jot down the reference information as you search and read articles rather than trying to come back to these websites days later, when you have to retrace your steps and try to remember where you found your information!

An annotated bibliography is a research tool made for this point in your writing process. It includes the reference for your source, with all the information you (or your reader) needs to find that source again, and a short, one-paragraph summary of the article—so you remember later what that one was all about.

This keeps you from wasting time looking for old websites, trying to remember if this was the article that had the great quote you want, or if it's really about something all together different. It saves you from rereading articles!

> SAMPLE ANNOTATED BIBLIOGRAPHY ENTRY:
>
> Brown, R. (2007) How To Study Smart Not Hard. Short & Sweet Books, Brooklyn, NY.
>
> This book teaches how to use study skills to speed learning and improve comprehension.

So, when you come to a source you think you *might* want to use in your paper, write down the author, title, publication date, today's date, and the URL where you found it. Then read it, and write a one-paragraph synopsis of the article. Mention whatever about that particular article you think is useful.

Then go on to your next article.

When you finish writing your paper and it's time to write the dreaded reference page,

Writing A Papers

you've already got it done! What? That's right, your annotated bibliography *is* your reference page, once you take out the annotations (that one paragraph synopsis you wrote for each entry). Also, remove any articles that you didn't end up using in your paper.

This method will also ensure that you don't accidentally plagiarize any data in your paper—a terrible thing to happen to a good student who is trying to do the right thing.

Avoiding Plagiarism & Copyright Infringement

One of the great benefits of the Internet is the freely available materials and information for your reading and knowledge. But for some reason, because so much information is easy to access and read, students have begun to think that it is also okay to copy and past these writings and pictures into their papers and posts. ***It is not.***

If You Think "Plagiarism isn't that Big a Deal"

You're wrong! Plagiarism is rampant in on-line school (as well as on-ground school) probably because it's such a temptation to merely copy a beautifully written scholarly paper and paste it into your own blank document. It's exactly what your professor asked for in your assignment, and you certainly couldn't write that well, so what's the harm?

There are a number of harms, including receiving an F on the assignment, being kicked out of school, and being prosecuted for criminal copyright infringement.

Just because you **can** copy something from an Internet source and paste it into your document, doesn't mean you **should**. Indeed, if you copy some things you will not only be in violation of plagiarism but of federal copyright laws—a criminal offense!

Avoiding Plagiarism & Copyright Infringement

THE TRUTH ABOUT PLAGIARISM:

If you copy someone else's words and sentences, rather than writing your own words and sentences	...	You aren't learning anything
If you copy and pretend that a paper, or a paragraph, or a sentence is your own	...	You are lying
If you don't put quote marks around any sentence or collection of words that you copy from another writer (whether from a book, website, article, or even a post)	...	You are stealing
If you turn in a paper that includes large amounts of text or even ideas that are not your own, and for which you do not indicate another author	...	You are cheating
Do colleges take these kinds of infractions seriously?	...	You bet they do!

If You Think "Nobody Will Ever Know if I Plagiarize"

You're wrong again! I catch students plagiarizing almost every day.

Professors Can Tell

I can tell if a paper is plagiarized by the change in the student's writing, by the use of words most students don't use, by the polish of professional writing as compared to student writing.

Remember, your professors teach this stuff. They can tell when they're reading something written by a professional in the field, another scholar or academic, or that a copy editor has carefully worked with.

Professors Check Up on You

Whenever I read a sentence that strikes me as particularly fine—I am suspicious. I run the sentence through Google search. You would be surprised at how many students don't realize that if they can run a Google search

Avoiding Plagiarism & Copyright Infringement

and come up with an article, I can run the same search and find the article they used!

I also use professional tools online for professors to help them catch plagiarizing. Turnitin.com is a website that allows professors to upload all the student papers, run a plagiarism report, and send back an email telling the professor what percentage of each paper was plagiarized. Turnitin.com even highlights the plagiarized sentences and phrases, and tells the professor where the student got those sentences.

So please do not copy any text, images, maps, sounds or ideas from the Internet and use them in your writing or even for your personal use on your computer. It is illegal and unethical.

If You Think "Nothing Really Happens if I Plagiarize or Copy Illegally"

Wrong again! The schools I work for to take plagiarism very seriously and they require me to take it seriously too. I have to hand out zeros for the assignment and report the student to the school administrators.

Not Knowing the Difference Won't Help

Saying "I didn't know" won't help you if you are caught plagiarizing, even if it is your first time. You're required to learn and understand the rules of plagiarism during your first class.

If you are caught plagiarizing, the least that will happen is you'll get a zero on the assignment. The worst is that this offense will go into your permanent record, you will be kicked out of school, and any other school you apply to will see that you are a plagiarizer.

Don't Take the Risk!

So if you think you can fool the system, you are playing with fire. Even if you manage to fool your professors some of the time, you won't fool them all of the time. It only takes one zero on a single assignment to drop your grade for the course below an A. The second instance of plagiarism **in your entire college career** will result in expulsion.

Avoiding Plagiarism & Copyright Infringement

If You Think "All I Have to Do is Put a Link in My Paper Somewhere"

Nope, that's not right either! In your research and writing for school, you must clearly attribute the words and **ideas** of others when you use them in your projects and papers.

That means putting quote marks around any sentences or paragraphs in your papers that you copy from others, and providing a reference so the reader knows where those words came from. Even if you just use someone else's idea, you have to provide a citation in your paper so your reader knows that wasn't your original idea.

Plagiarism and how to quote, paraphrase and cite your sources are a complicated system, but you'll have to learn it. Your school and many online sources also have wonderful tutorials to teach you what you can and cannot do. I suggest you use them.

If you already know what to do and what not to do, here is a short list of points you can check with every paper to make sure you haven't plagiarized:

> Plagiarism Checklist:
>
> 1. Did you include a reference page or Works Cited page at the end of your paper?
> 2. Did you put quote marks around any sentence or partial sentence that you copied exactly from your source?
> 3. Did you include an in-text citation immediately follow that quote?
> 4. Did you include an in-text citation immediately following anyplacce you paraphrased your source?
> 5. Have you made sure that not more than 10% of your paper is a direct quote?

MLA & APA Styles

finally, your paper is written, you've been careful not to plagiarize, you've proofread it all and you're ready to turn it in. But wait! You have to format it according to the correct style for your department.

Say what?

I remember when I was a freshman in college getting ready to turn in my first paper, and my professor mentioned that there was a style sheet that we had to use for our papers. I couldn't understand what he was talking about? A style sheet? What was that? I'd checked the spelling, I'd put my name on it, I'd printed it off, what more was there?

I simply couldn't get my head around this idea that different departments would have different rules about how to format a paper: the width of margins, where the title and my name go, how to cite my sources. Not only that, but they seemed to be **serious** about enforcing those rules.

Yes, they really are! In many schools, your professors simply won't accept a paper that isn't formatted correctly. And in many professions, the same is true. I knew an attorney who had his claim returned to him by the judge because his margins were not correct on his documents!

What Are Styles?

A style is how a publisher or institution requires that your paper be formatted for them. It also includes what sort of information you must have in your references, whether you must have a title page, whether to use footnotes or endnotes.

Really, anything having to do with the choices you make about how your paper looks, is in these style sheet rules. And you thought those decisions were up to you!

The Two Primary College Styles

There are two main styles that you are likely to encounter in your online school (although you should be aware that there are at least seven other styles that are used in this country). Those two main styles are MLA and APA. Most English departments use MLA. Most social science and business departments use APA.

I am not going to go over the particulars here, because they are very detailed and often slightly different at each college. (Sigh . . . yes, I know. Could they make this any harder on the students?)

Ask Your Professor for the Style

What you have to do is ask your professor for the style sheet, or the manual that her department recommends. Then when you're ready to turn in your paper, go through that sheet point by point and make sure you are following the style exactly!

That's the way we all do it, even the professionals. So no moaning and groaning— this is just a fact of life.

Available Online Resources

Oh, but wait! I almost forgot. There's an online tool that will help you. That's right, there is an online tool called the Citation Machine. It won't format your entire paper, but it will format those citations and references that are so irritatingly difficult to do right.

Go to www.citationmachine.net.

On the left hand side of your screen you will see a menu for MLA, APA, and Chicago. Choose the style that you're required to use, and then fill in the boxes with the data that's asked for and click the button. The Citation Machine will spit out a perfect in-text citation and reference for your paper. You can just copy and paste it.

So that speeds up *that* process!!

There are all kinds of other online resources that will help you with everything about writing a paper, including style sheets, citations, grammar and punctuation. For a list, please see the appendix in this book.

In Closing . . .

I hope that now you have a much better understanding of how college works in general, and how Internet colleges work in particular. Knowledge is power, and I expect you to put this new power to use immediately to improve your grades in all your classes.

Return to this book as you need it; if you run into problems with an instructor, it would be helpful to review how professors evaluate their students and what your best methods for dealing with your professor might be.

Don't think like a student—think like an adult! Think about your goal, earning that degree and getting the best grades while you do it, and then decide on your course of action.

When writing papers or studying textbooks, you might want to refresh your memory about the Fast Sheets and Smart Notes. You'll have to practice these a few times before they come easily and naturally to you.

Finally, don't forget that college is about learning and improving. So take every criticism, every comment from a professor or classmate as a valuable insight into how you might improve. That's what the A students are doing.

And now that you're one of that crowd, I know you'll be doing it too!

Good studying!

Appendixes

Appendix A: CHEA Recognized Accrediting Organizations as of 2006

Regional Accrediting Organizations

- Middle States Association of Colleges and Schools Middle States Commission on Higher Education
- New England Association of Schools and Colleges Commission on Institutions of Higher Education
- New England Association of Schools and Colleges Commission on Technical and Career Institutions
- North Central Association of Colleges and Schools The Higher Learning Commission
- Northwest Commission on Colleges and Universities
- Southern Association of Colleges and Schools commission on Colleges
- Western Association of Schools and Colleges Accrediting Commission for Community and Junior Colleges
- Western Association of Schools and Colleges Accrediting Commission for Senior Colleges and Universities

Faith-Based Accrediting Organizations

- Association for Biblical Higher Education Commission on Accreditation
- Association of Advanced Rabbinical and Talmudic Schools Accreditation Commission
- Commission on Accreditation of the Association of Theological Schools in the United States and Canada
- Transnational Association of Christian Colleges and Schools Accreditation Commission

Private Career Accrediting Organizations

- Accrediting Council of Independent Colleges and Schools
- Distance Education and Training Council Accrediting Commission

To be sure you are looking at an updated list of CHEA recognized accrediting organization, please go to the CHEA website: http://www.chea.org/search/default.asp

Appendix B: Glossary of Terms

Accelerated classes – An entire semester's worth of assignments crammed into 5-10 short weeks.

Annotated bibliography – A research tool made for this point in your writing process. It includes the reference for your source, with all the information you (or your reader) needs to find that source again, and a short, one-paragraph summary of the article—so you remember later what that one was all about.

APA style – A particular way of formatting your paper before you turn it in. There are two main styles that you are likely to encounter in your online school (although you should be aware that there are at least seven other styles that are used in this country). They are MLA and APA. Most English departments use MLA. Most social science and business departments use APA.

Assignment calendar – A calendar that you create by noting when each assignment is due, and when you need to complete each *part* of that assignment. Having this will make sure you stay on schedule for everything you have to turn in.

Asynchronous – Courses never require that you be online at the same time as anyone else in your class, including your instructor. The beauty of asynchronous courses is that you really can do that work any time during the day that you can fit it in. Even if that is in the middle of the night.

Attaching documents - When you turn in a paper or other document to your professor for grading, you will have to attach that paper to your post to send it. Attaching just means that when you send the post to the school's server, a copy of the paper goes along with it.

Most software programs allow you to attach a document by clicking on a button that says "Attach" or on a little paperclip icon. Once you click on that button, a window will open up allowing you to type in the name of the document or find it on your computer.

Bulletin board – A board usually made of cork that you stick notes to will a pin. Also, a space on the school's computer where you post messages to your professors and classmates. Classes are conducted on newsgroup, which are also called message boards or bulletin boards. Newsgroups work very much like a real bulletin board. People post notes on the bulletin board and other people read those notes and post replies.

Copyright – A legal right everyone has as soon as they create something. If

Appendix B: Glossary

you copy what someone else has created, you have infringed their copyright. A criminal offense!

Course load – How many classes you are allowed (or required) to take at once. For online schools, this is usually not more than two.

Discussion questions (DQs) – Questions about the materials that your professor posts for you and your classmates to discuss. Talking about these ideas helps you learn and understand them better.

Distance education – Also known as online universities and eCollege, is a method of delivering college-level programs and courses to students who cannot sit in the same physical classroom as their instructors.

eCollege - Going to college online. Also, a web-based platform that some online universities use to deliver their class materials.

eMail - Messages that you send from your computer over the Internet.

Excel – A software program from Microsoft Office Suite that allows you to make spreadsheets on your computer.

Fast Sheets – Becky Brown's system for compiling your notes into handy cards that you can easily use when you study or write papers.

Grade Point Average (GPA) – The grade you are earning. GPA is calculated by adding all the grades you've earned in each class and dividing the sum by the total of classes you've taken. Also, you can figure out your GPA (and so your grade) in any class by adding all the points you've earned so far, and dividing that sum by the number of points *it is possible* to earn so far.

Grievance - The official record you file (or is filed against you) for wrong behavior in the classroom. Your professor can file a grievance against you for misbehaving, and you can file a grievance against your professor for giving you an unfair grade.

Helpdesk – The place you call whenever you have problems with the software or hardware, including not being able to access your class, forgetting your password, changing your login name, etc.

Individual newsgroups (ING) - A bulletin board that only you and your professor can see.

Informative paper - A paper that merely presents the facts and not an opinion.

Internet technology (IT) - Everything having to do with software, hardware and the Internet. The IT people man the helpdesk, and help you when you have problems with these things.

Appendix B: Glossary

Late policy - The policy your professor enforces about when you can turn in late assignments, and how many points you lose if they're late.

Message boards (MB) – Classes are conducted on newsgroup, which are also called message boards or bulletin boards. Newsgroups work very much like a real bulletin board. People post notes on the bulletin board and other people read those notes and post replies.

Microsoft Word (MSWord) – The standard word processing program required in every online university. It is not the same thing as Microsoft Works, WordPerfect, or Notepad.

MLA style – A particular way of formatting your paper before you turn it in. There are two main styles that you are likely to encounter in your online school (although you should be aware that there are at least seven other styles that are used in this country). They are MLA and APA. Most English departments use MLA. Most social science and business departments use APA.

Newsgroups (NG) - Classes are conducted on newsgroup, which are also called message boards or bulletin boards. Newsgroups work very much like a real bulletin board. People post notes on the bulletin board and or newsgroup, it's called "posting" the message.

Posts - Messages on bulletin boards or newsgroups are called "posts."

PowerPoint – Software from the Microsoft Office Suite that businesses use to create visual presentations.

Smart Notes – Becky Brown's system of reading and taking notes that speeds your studying and ensures that you actually learn the material.

Style sheets - A particular way of formatting your paper before you turn it in. There are two main styles that you are likely to encounter in your online school (although you should be aware that there are at least 10 other styles that are used in this country). They are MLA and APA. Most English departments use MLA. Most social science and business departments use APA.

Syllabus – The contract between you and your professor. The syllabus tells you what your professor expects from you during the class, and what you can expect from your professor.

Synchronous - courses require students to meet online at a scheduled time each week. During these meetings faculty and students meet in a chat room where they can "talk" in real time. Faculty usually have lessons planned, which often include visual aids like movies, podcasts

Appendix B: Glossary 159

other people read those notes and post replies.

On-ground school – Traditional classes that are held in a brick and mortar classroom, with a professor standing in front of you.

Online school – Classes that are held on a website or other Internet software. Your professor and your classmates are all in different locations and often never even meet in real time.

Outlook Express (OE) – Software from the Microsoft Office Suite that collects and sends email, and lets you access your newsgroups. Some schools use OE to conduct their online classes.

Paper criteria list - A list you write of all the requirements you have to be sure your paper meets.

Persuasive paper - A paper that makes a claim and supports that claim with data. An argument.

Plagiarism - Taking the words or ideas of another author and passing them off as your own. Forgetting to put quote marks around a quote, and forgetting to provide the citation and reference are considered plagiarism.

Posting - Posting is how you get messages that you write on your computer up to the school's computer. When you put a message on a bulletin board and PowerPoint presentations. Students get to really meet their classmates, exchange comments, questions, and greetings, and get immediate responses from their instructors

Tone – The words and ideas you convey in your messages to your professor and your classmates. Be careful that you always use a professional tone. This is a public space, and anything you write in class can be read by all your classmates, all their friends, and the administration of the school.

Appendix C: Online Resources

You are among the first generation of college students to have the vast resources of the Internet available to you for all sortss of research. So learn to turn there first when you are confused.

Below are a list of some of my favorite writing, studying and grammar websites. Sometimes you need a tutorial to help you understand, sometimes just reading about it in different words will make the lightbulb go on. So give these websites a shot.

How to Write A Five-paragraph paper

These website include great discussions and tutorials about how to write a five-paragraph paper. The building-block of all papers.

>   *http://www.gc.maricopa.edu/English/writing.html*
>   *http://www.geocities.com/jk102.geo*

http://essayinfo.com/essays/5-paragraph_essay.php

http://www.englishdiscourse.org/5.paragraph.essay.format.htm

How to Write Thesis Statements

These are great places to get help with your thesis statement.

http://www.wisc.edu/writing/Handbook/Thesis.html

http://www.rpi.edu/web/writingcenter/thesis.html

http://www.indiana.edu/~wts/pamphlets/thesis_statement.shtml

http://leo.stcloudstate.edu/acadwrite/thesistatement.html

http://www.unc.edu/depts/wcweb/handouts/thesis

Help With APA Style

Citation Machine

http://www.citationmachine.net

If you gather the data, this online tool with format the citations and references for you!

APA Style

http://www.apastyle.org/
The official website of APA Style

The OWL at Purdue

http://owl.english.purdue.edu/owl/resource/560/01/

Help with MLA Style

Citation Machine

http://www.citationmachine.net
This works for MLA style too!

The Owl at Purdue

http://owl.english.purdue.edu/owl/resource/557/01/MSWord Tutorials

MSWord Help

If you need help learning to use your MSWord program, there are a number of free, online tutorials for you to use. Here are a few I like:

http://www.bcschools.net/staff/WordHelp.htm
http://office.microsoft.com/en-us/training/CR061832731033.aspx
http://www.internet4classrooms.com/on-line_word.htm
http://www.learnthat.com/courses/computer/word/
http://netforbeginners.about.com/od/learnmsword/Learn_Microsoft_Word_97_2000_2002_2003.htm

PowerPoint Help

PowerPoint skills to the most complex. They can be found at:

Appendix C: Online Resources

http://office.microsoft.com/en-us/training/CR061832731033.aspx http://www.bcschools.net/staff/PowerPointHelp.htm

Excel Help

But for you more math-inclined students, you'll find Excel is your best friend. Use it wisely—learn the program! Here are tutorials that I hear are quite good:

http://www.usd.edu/trio/tut/excel/
http://www.fgcu.edu/support/office2000/excel/
http://www.bcschools.net/staff/ExcelHelp.htm

Where to Get Instant Messaging Software

You just have to know their IM name. (Mine is ProfBecky. You can IM me too!)

http://www.aim.com/index.adp

About The Author

Rebecca Brown, M.A., has taught more than 3000 courses online. She teaches English, humanities and critical thinking courses. Becky also tutors students in study skills and paper writing.

Becky is the author of several Short & Sweet Book titles, including **HOW TO STUDY SMART NOT HARD**, and **HOW TO MAKE As in eCOLLEGE**, which can be found at http://*www.ShortandSweetBooks.com*.

She loves to talk to students about their on-line school experiences and is always happy to answer questions, help with problems, and applaud successes in the eCollege world.

If you would like to be tutored by Becky, or take one of her study skills seminars please email her at:

BeckyBrown@ShortandSweetBooks.com

www.ingramcontent.com/pod-product-compliance
Lightning Source LLC
Chambersburg PA
CBHW032256150426
43195CB00008BA/481